Contact Info:

I would love to hear from you regarding your Goodness Campaign. Here are some ideas and questions to get you started. Feel free to add your own!

- Has this book changed your perspective? If so, how?
- How have you incorporated the principles and ideas in the book with your beliefs and lifestyle?
- How do you plan to live with more goodness?
- Will you volunteer additional time, tolerance, money, or kindness?
- How are you taking care?
- Have you been able to apologize to others and clear some of your conscience pests?
- Have you forgiven someone and improved your quality of life?
- Did you improve emotional, spiritual, or physical health?
- Do you offer more respect and care for nature and our environment?

Please reply at thegoodnesscampaign.com
ORDER INFO:

The Goodness Campaign…getting back to good can be purchased online at www.thegoodnesscampaign.com and ordered at finer bookstores everywhere! Thanks for taking the time to make a difference! I hope to meet you soon and learn about your Goodness Campaign!!

GOD IS GRACE

Lessons to a Father from a Son

By Warren Bolton

Foreword by Tanya Bolton

authorHOUSE®

AuthorHouse™
1663 Liberty Drive
Bloomington, IN 47403
www.authorhouse.com
Phone: 1-800-839-8640

First published by AuthorHouse   12/02/2011

ISBN: 978-1-4685-0673-0 (sc)
ISBN: 978-1-4685-0674-7 (hc)
ISBN: 978-1-4685-0671-6 (ebk)

Library of Congress Control Number: 2011961318

Printed in the United States of America

* All Scripture references are from the King James Version of the Bible.

Manuscript Editor: Bertram Rantin

Table of Contents

Foreword

Being a mother is both the most difficult and most rewarding job I've ever had. It's a constant balancing act—work, family, church, and whatever else presents itself. And like most parents, I have to remember that despite the many balls I have to keep in the air, my primary job is to be a good parent. Someone who cares and provides for, nurtures, protects, and is ultimately responsible for the overall well-being of their precious children. Someone who puts their needs second to ensure their children grow into healthy, productive citizens.

To say the least, parenting is the job you can't get paid enough for; you never get to clock out (not even for sick days); and there are sure to be heartaches. But with hard work, lots of prayer and perseverance, you are more likely to rear children who bring you great joy and pride.

As a mother and licensed professional counselor, I have found that children tend to mirror what they've been exposed to. Yes, they will come up with words, phrases, and behaviors that will make you question where in the world they heard or saw that. But, on average, what you see and hear from your children is a reflection of you.

Their dominant traits and behaviors, coping styles, perspectives on life and other topics, and self-image are most often formed based on how we, as parents, interact with them, the rest of our family and others in society.

I'll be the first to acknowledge that I have struggles as a parent. Some days, I wonder if I've said the right thing; if I've encouraged our two boys enough; if I've been a good example in how I reacted to a situation verbally and in terms of my behavior. I worry that I didn't encourage them enough or didn't prepare them enough for possible negative events of the day.

As a licensed counselor whose job is to encourage and help prepare people to live happier, healthier, more fulfilling lives, I have to make sure that I'm that advocate for my children too. That is a full-time job that requires even more than I—or you, when it comes to your children—gave at the office. But I give 100 percent to others. Why not do the same or more for the children I prayed for and promised God I would care for, protect, and prepare for a bright, productive future?

As I read this book, I smiled because it reflected so many wonderful memories and realizations. I remembered the stories Warren shares about Alexander's compassionate spirit, even as a younger child, and how his keen sense of discernment caused him to reach out to and encourage strangers. He still does that today. His methods have changed some as he's gotten older, but he's still intuitive and purposeful in sharing God's love and encouragement.

And he's being a great big brother to Christopher, who adores Alexander. Christopher is more of a brute, as I call him teasingly. He considers himself a dinosaur—just like his big brother—and takes every opportunity to growl and chase nearby children after identifying himself as a T-Rex. He's an awesome T-Rex, too.

And like Alexander, Christopher walks around singing songs of praise, praying for our family and others, and inquiring about how to heal the world. I'm proud to see our children developing a strong foundation in the Lord. Even so, I still ask myself and God what else I can do.

What's clear, though, is that we've at least done a few things right. We've taught them to pray and allowed them to develop their own prayers; we've taught them God's word and given examples of how it applies to daily situations; we show love to each other and to them. I'm glad some of our lessons are bearing fruit even at their young ages. But there's so much more to teach them.

I pray that you read this book and are encouraged to stay focused on God and establish a solid foundation in His Word for yourself and your children. Work diligently to teach your children godly lessons needed for basic survival. And I pray that you see God's blessings in your life, your family members' lives, and all you cover in prayer. As you grow in Christ, help lead others to Him.

Thanks to the author, my husband, for being so wonderful, loving and supportive. I only hope our sons will be as awesome as you, Warren! I always prayed that God would bless me with someone as godly and wonderful (and powerful) as my maternal grandfather, McKinley "Diggy" Brown. He did! Diggy loved you, my mom loves you, and most of all, I adore you! I look forward to many more years with you and our boys.

Tanya E. Bolton, MA, LPC, CAC
President, Bolton Counseling & Consulting, LLC

I thank God, our Father, for His divine guidance, Alexander, my tiny theologian, for his inspiration and my wife, Tanya, and youngest son, Christopher, for their love and devotion.

Photo by JEROME P. BRYANT

The Boltons (left to right):
Christopher, Tanya, Alexander and Warren

Introduction

The trip home from the hospital in 2005 after the birth of our first son, Alexander, was the longest, most careful ride of my life. My wife, Tanya, was both traffic cop and protective mother as she guarded our precious cargo. I had to drive at the right speed, stay the proper distance behind the car ahead of me, and make precise turns—or else. If it even appeared as if other drivers were going to take a chance at a light or stop sign as we were crossing an intersection, they got a new mother's icy cold stare. Our safe arrival home was a time of relief and celebration. We would repeat that same long, careful ride in 2008 after the birth of our youngest son, Christopher.

In each case, the ride was just beginning. Today, Alexander is 6 and Christopher is 3, and they can be as challenging as any other active little boys. We know that God blessed and entrusted us with them and has equipped us with what we need to raise God-fearing, obedient, loving boys with a drive to succeed.

You'd think that two professionals—my wife is a licensed professional counselor who has many children as clients and I'm a minister and journalist—would be able to raise balanced, godly children with ease. But regardless of who we are, we all have to figure out child-rearing; kids don't come with instructions, as they say.

As I have taught, encouraged and, yes, disciplined Alexander and Christopher, I have often noticed a parallel in how God treats me as His child. I find myself offering grace in instances where I clearly don't want to. They've done something so egregious (in my mind) that it deserves the toughest kind of punishment.

But then I think about how God has treated me, how God has let me off the hook so many times. And I'm compelled to do the same for my sons. I consider how God must think about some of the things I've done in my life. Did He condemn me? Thank goodness not. As a matter of fact, He loved me so much that He sent His son to suffer, bleed and die for me—and the entire world, including my boys.

Thank God for His grace.

I see my relationship with the Father so much more clearly as I interact with my boys.

They depend on me wholly, to the point that their very lives and the very quality of their lives depends on me and their mother. My life and its quality, likewise, depend totally on God.

When the boys do something that puts them in danger or causes them to hurt, sometimes I want to chastise them. But I'm often forced to see it as God sees it, respond to them as God responds to me. Yes, He brings correction, but He also brings healing, restoration and reassurance. Above all, He often protects me and anticipates my shortcomings and my impending stumbling and bumbling. I find myself anticipating my boys' next move and trying to move things out of their way or give them due warning of what's ahead.

I get frustrated sometimes at what I'm called to do for them, but I know God never gives up on me and I, in turn, am called on never to give up on my children.

In many ways, I know I am the first semblance of God they will see. It's through me that they will learn much about the Father—through my teaching them His words and His ways both through His word and through my actions. They're going to learn most through how I treat them, how I treat their mother, how I treat God and how I treat others.

So often, situations arise with them and I think: "That's the way God sees me."

I imagine God saying, "Didn't I tell you that wouldn't work?" "Why are you always getting yourself in these predicaments?" "You just won't learn will you?" "If you are obedient, I will reward you." "Didn't I tell you no?" "Didn't I say not yet?" "Didn't I say wait?"

So, I've learned to embrace my role as a father and the demands and expectations that come with it. After all, I do expect God to be the benevolent, understanding, forgiving provider and Father that He is. God expects and demands no less from me; my sons expect no less of me.

I'm not the perfect father, but I'm striving every day to be better at it than I was the previous day. Indeed, I embrace the fact that these two little boys depend on me and need me to help them in every aspect of their lives.

I'm learning more and more to embrace the fruit of the spirit—love, joy, peace, longsuffering, gentleness, goodness, faith, meekness and self control. If you've got children, you need every element of the fruit of the spirit every day, just as God exhibits those toward us.

And yet, even as I embrace my role as father, I've been astounded that I learn as much from my sons, Alexander in particular, as I teach them. While helping me become the father I need to be, Alexander has also opened my eyes to a deeper understanding of the Everlasting Father.

In his own way—unbeknownst to him—Alexander has strengthened my faith and challenged me to draw closer to God. I certainly have grown much and can more readily admit that I have even more growing to do, all because of what God imparted to me through my son.

I share these experiences and exchanges between me and Alexander in hopes that other fathers and mothers might be open to what God is saying to them through their children.

Chapter 1

'God Is Grace'

"For by grace are ye saved through faith; and not of

yourselves; it is the gift of God; Not of works,

lest any man should boast."

Ephesians 2:8-9

We should have known it the night he was born.

Upon his arrival on this life-supporting sphere God so graciously shaped, formed and stocked for us, Alexander

1

wasted no time in signaling that he was special beyond the fact he was our first born. Promptly after the doctor had pulled him from his mother's womb a nurse took him to a table to suction him and clear his passage ways. She had no sooner laid him down when he turned his head and looked at us—he could see clearly. Ever since, he's seen with an unusual clarity and has blessed me as he's allowed me to see God in a very different, very special, deep way.

While I cherish my personal walk with the Lord, it's been refreshing and humbling to see him through a child's eyes. The prayers Alexander lifts heavenward are so pure, so genuine, and so effective.

I understand now more than ever what Jesus meant when He said that those who come to the kingdom must come as children.

When Alexander was a mere toddler, he would surprise us by his insight. My wife, Tanya, tells the story of the day they were out shopping and they saw this woman who appeared to be troubled. They passed her several times as they shopped. Eventually, my wife and Alexander spoke. Alexander then extended his hand and told the woman everything was going to be all right. She told my wife she needed to hear that. She was going through a tough time.

Other very similar things have happened with Alexander over the years. He would be drawn to mere strangers and sense that they had a void or some challenge they were dealing with and would say or do what eventually proved to be just the right thing. There was the day in a local deli when he hugged a man he didn't know who had been dealing with some personal issues. This grown man broke down and cried as this little boy reached out and loved.

There also was the time when, as a kindergartener in public school, Alexander noticed a faculty member was hobbling on a leg. He asked what had happened. When she told him about her problem leg, he told her that "at my old school, (a private school operated by our church, Bethel A.M.E. in Columbia, S.C.) we would pray and say 'in the name of Jesus be healed.'" She was struck by his boldness and caring heart. She told him she felt better already. She would later tell my wife that she appreciated that someone was still teaching their children to have faith in God.

Who said there is no more prayer in school? Instill it in your children and they'll take it wherever they go.

We enrolled Alexander into our church's child development center at age 2. As is the case with church-run schools, they taught the children to say grace. The one he learned at age 3 was a very familiar one:

> *God is great, God is good.*
> *Let us thank Him for our food.*
> *By His hand we all are fed.*
> *Give us Lord our daily bread.*
> *Amen, thank you Lord.*

But when Alexander led us in the grace at home, he never said, "God is great." It was always, "God is grace."

Indeed He is.

Grace is an amazing gift from God. God's relationship toward us is steeped in grace. "For by grace are ye saved through faith; and not of yourselves; it is the gift of God; Not of works, lest any man should boast." (Ephesians 2:8-9)

When he first began saying the word "grace" instead of "great," I wanted to correct Alexander. But the Holy Spirit wouldn't allow me. Instead of *correcting* him, I needed to *receive from* him.

Alexander might as well have been saying: "God is unmerited favor. You don't deserve His love. You don't deserve His forgiveness. You don't even deserve this food. But for the grace of God your plate would be empty and your cupboard bare."

I think a lot about grace these days. Grace in a secular sense is a real big deal right about now. People's credit cards are maxed out, mortgages are past due, credit lines have been shut down. Many people are late on their bills and are taking full advantage of the grace period creditors extend with the hope that those who haven't paid will do so.

God's grace operates somewhat similar but so much more perfectly and heavenly. The grace extended by credit card companies or other creditors runs out. They might give you 15 or even 30 days. Their purpose is expressly to give you time to pay, often without penalty. But when your time is up, it's up. Penalties apply. Pressure is applied. Leniency takes flight.

But God's grace is so much more. It's a supernatural outpouring that fits you and your situation just right. It's an extension of God's goodness—of His protection and love and, ultimately, of the Father himself. God's grace is His total, unconditional embrace of sinful, undeserving man.

Above all, God's grace is sufficient. It isn't bound by time or circumstances or the nature and quantity of your sins. It can't be, because God isn't. And God is grace.

In as much as God's grace is unmerited favor, it not only can result in the extension of time, but of so much more. It comes with no strings attached and isn't subject to be cancelled. God's big like that.

There's nothing that we can do to earn the salvation that God extends to us through Jesus Christ. There's no amount of money we could present or work we could do to earn salvation. We receive salvation, not because of who we are or who our parents are or what position we hold in the church or community, but because God simply loves us and covers all our debt, all our sin with his everlasting love.

But, like credit card companies, God expects us to do something—to take advantage of that grace. He's extending us time and opportunity to be saved, to get our houses in order, to set things right, to become the saints that He expects us to be.

Upon seeing someone homeless or in a bad predicament, many of us are heard to utter: "But for the grace of God there go I."

If that be the case, then God expects us to respond to that grace that has allowed us to escape sure death and destruction. Do something. If God saved you, if He kept you out of or even brought you out of a bad situation, what are you going to do to help another person come out? What are you going to do to ease their pain? To help them overcome?

Indeed, God is grace. Coming from the lips of a child, could it be just a slip of the tongue? Could it be just by happenstance that Alexander said "grace" instead of "great?" By the way, he's still praying it although he knows how most of us recite the grace. And Christopher is following in his big brother's footsteps.

I know God well enough to not question why Alexander ever began saying the grace the way he does. Instead, my question has been: "Lord, what is it that you want this child to teach me? What is it that I'm supposed to learn?"

Sometimes, I think it's a reminder that as God's grace has fallen upon me, so should my grace—as paltry as it is—fall upon my children as well as others. I shouldn't be so fixated on being the hard-line disciplinarian that I forget that a father—like "the Father"—must have the capacity to extend grace.

And in being reminded that "God is grace," I should be cognizant that as God has shed His grace on me, so should I extend grace to others.

Chapter 2

'Keep Us Safe For A Holy Nation'

"But ye are a chosen generation, a royal priesthood,

an holy nation, a peculiar people; that ye should

shew forth the praises of him who hath called you

out of darkness into his marvelous light."

1 Peter 2:9

Every morning, Tanya, Alexander, Christopher and I come together in prayer before we leave home. We also pray with each of our children at bedtime. About 90 percent of the time, Alexander leads us in prayer, and oftentimes he starts out by saying, "God, keep us safe for a holy nation."

The first time I heard him say that I chuckled and, you guessed it, wanted to correct him. I wanted to tell him how and what to pray. But the Lord opened my eyes on that. The more I heard him pray it, the more the Lord dealt with me about being holy and working to become all that He desires us to be. "Because it is written, Be ye holy; for I am holy." (1 Peter 1:16) Or as God said to Abram in Genesis 17:1b, "I am the Almighty God; walk before me, and be thou perfect." That command came with a promise in Genesis 17:2: "And I will make my covenant between me and thee, and will multiply thee exceedingly."

The more Alexander prayed "God, keep us safe for a holy nation," the more I was forced to ponder its meaning. Why should God keep us safe for a holy nation? As I meditated on it, I came to understand that the only real reason for God to keep us safe each and every day, the only reason for Him to take us out and bring us back home safely, the only reason for His favor and anointing to rest upon us constantly is to preserve us as a nation holy unto Himself, a nation that goes forth and does the will and work of the Father and gives Him the honor and glory He is due. The only reason for God to allow us to see His goodness in the land of the living one more day is for us to carry out His purpose and promise for our lives. He wants us to be examples, to be witnesses, to share the gospel, to be His representatives in the earth.

What's a holy nation? It's a people—not necessarily in one church body but a broader congregation—bound together by

God's spirit, one governed by God's principles, and given, quite frankly, to living a life that is pleasing to God—no matter what.

God expects us every day to know who we are and to act like we know who we are. We're expected to act like members of a royal priesthood, in what we say and what we do and what we think. We're expected to carry ourselves in contradiction to the world; when God says be ye holy as I am holy, he means it. He expects us to strive for holiness.

Impossible, right? Then why would God command it without wavering? Anything He tells or commands us to do is possible—not because we're so able—but because He's so able. He will equip the saints and empower them to succeed. "Being confident of this very thing, that he which hath begun a good work in you will perform it until the day of Jesus Christ." (Philippians 1:6)

We're called out by God to be set apart, sanctified. To be sanctified doesn't indicate that you're part of a certain denomination, as so many of us thought growing up. It's a lifestyle and condition brought on by the work and power of the Holy Spirit.

God wants His people to be sanctified, cleansed from the inside out. It's not about the length of your dress or the amount of makeup you wear or whether you wear a certain kind or amount of jewelry. It's about allowing the Holy Spirit to move toward completing a good work in you. It's about putting off the old and putting on the new. It's about getting the junk out and Jesus in.

2 Corinthians 5:17 tells us that, "Therefore if any man be in Christ, he is a new creature; old things are passed away; behold, all things are become new." If we are in Christ, there is an expectation—no, an assurance—that a transformation will take place, one that dispenses with the old and what used to be and introduces or ushers in something new and wondrous. I love that word "behold." It says stop, look, listen, check it out. In other words, people ought to be able to see the transformation. They should be able to observe the difference in the life of one walking with Jesus.

Most importantly, it suggests that the one going through the transformation can attain to it and that they will witness the transformation within themselves, which will equip them to become witnesses to others. That's why 2 Corinthians 5 goes on to say that believers become ministers of reconciliation and ambassadors for Christ.

Holiness isn't an abstract concept. It's not simply to be talked about as if it's some mist or smoke that can't be captured or obtained. It's to be laid hold of and lived out. It's a lifestyle that is openly displayed and is so real that people readily see it. If you're "in Christ," people ought to see the stamp of Christ on you. Just as they see your car before you get out of it, they ought to see Christ first when you walk into a room. For all too many saints, reputations, protestations and other boisterous attributes arrive on a scene long before they—or the Christ in them—do. The result is a bad witness.

Don't get me wrong. Holiness does not arrive by some magical means. Hocus-pocus, abracadabra and other such gibberish will get you nowhere when it comes to holiness. It comes only by commitment, prayer, fasting, study and seeking God's guidance. This is something you've got to work at.

It's a process, and we won't all be at the same place at the same time. We are all growing at different paces. But our sanctification process should be ongoing. When we acknowledge Christ as savior, all of the old doesn't pass away overnight. We don't stop doing or saying everything we need to stop doing or saying at once.

Although some people might stop cussing immediately or even cease drunken, riotous living immediately, for many, the process is more gradual. We might be saved but the words that roll from our lips aren't the words of the saved; talk to us the wrong way and we'll cuss you out. We might be saved, but we still have the urge to touch or feel something a saved person shouldn't touch or feel. But keep on pressing on. God is not through with you yet.

Paul says in Philippians 3:14 that he is pressing "toward the mark for the prize of the high calling of God in Christ Jesus." So what's that high calling? Romans 12:1, 2 says, "I beseech you therefore, brethren, by the mercies of God, that ye present your bodies a living sacrifice, holy, acceptable unto God, which is your reasonable service. And be not conformed to this world; but be ye transformed by the renewing of your mind, that ye may prove what is that good, and acceptable, and perfect, will of God."

I know your next question: So what's the perfect will of God? Glad you asked. 1 Thessalonians 4:3a tells us: "For this is the will of God, even your sanctification . . ." In other words, it is God's desire that we be sanctified, set apart for his service. HOLY.

And He doesn't leave us to find our own way to holiness. He has designed a process and provided an agent of holiness—the Holy Spirit. As the Holy Spirit does His work in us, we'll begin to change. Hate and cheating and lying and sin will take a back seat to the fruit of the spirit: love, joy, peace, longsuffering, gentleness, goodness, faith, meekness and temperance (or self control).

In outlining the fruit of the spirit in Galatians 5:22-23, Paul says that "against such there is no law." When we walk in holiness and display the fruit of the spirit, there is no limit to our love, our longsuffering, our peace, our joy. We're not bound by any limitations. That's called freedom.

So, when Alexander prays, "Lord, keep us safe for a holy nation," I'm blessing God for the wisdom of my son's youth. All the mercies that God bestows upon us are purposeful. It's often not about us, but about how He wants to use us for His greater glory.

Our covering isn't because we have so much to offer or because we come from the right family, but because of our membership in a holy nation. If you're saved, a born again believer, this is who you are—or at least who you're supposed to be.

God wants you to know that if you're searching for an identity, if you're trying to find where you belong, you don't have to try to find yourself by joining some club or organization. You don't have to search for love and meaning in gangs or illicit drugs or promiscuous activity. Your meaning in life and your true identity isn't dependent on some man or woman.

While joining clubs and various social organizations is a good thing, and while they do some *good* work, it's not always *God* work. If you're itching to become a member of an extraordinary club but don't have the connections or the resources or the socio-political status, look no more. God's got a club for you. It's an extraordinary club that specializes in welcoming and elevating ordinary people.

Your age doesn't matter. Your socio-economic status doesn't matter. Your human pedigree doesn't matter. As a matter of fact, when you meet Jesus, He'll change your pedigree and will transfer your citizenship from this world to heaven.

Unfortunately, Christians spend too much time trying to be like the world. Trying to look like the world. Trying to climb the social ladder. Trying to climb the corporate ladder. Trying to climb the financial ladder. Trying to fit in with the world. Trying to get the world to like us. Trying to get the world to embrace us.

But the world didn't embrace Jesus: Remember, He's the one who came unto His own, and His own knew Him not. And the world won't embrace his followers.

If you choose Jesus, the world will seek to ridicule you, ostracize you, lock you out, stonewall you and thwart you.

But be of good courage, membership in God's supernaturally backed club has its privileges. God's club is backed by the full faith and credit of the Father. He has a health plan, a financial plan, a retirement plan and even a long-term care plan (heaven is our home) for His members. Not only is His warranty everlasting, but He made us to last forever and to rule and reign with Him.

When things get tough, we can go to the Father and access the privileges of our membership. We need only ask according to His will; we can confidently cite, chapter and verse, the promises and privileges God has provided us in His word: If you're sick, it might be Isaiah 53:5: "with his stripes we are healed." If you're under attack, it might be Isaiah 54:17: "No weapon that is formed against thee shall prosper . . ." If you're fearful, it might be 2 Timothy 1:7: "For God hath not given us the spirit of fear, but of power, and of love, and of a sound mind."

Matthew 6:33 tells us: "But seek ye first the kingdom of God, and his righteousness; and all these things shall be added unto you." In other words, set your Holy Ghost homepage on God, befriend God, Google God first. Make Him the center of your life. Set your affections on things above. Then, and only then, will all else—what you're going to eat, where you're going to sleep, what you're going to wear—follow.

We don't have to fret about situations and circumstances around us if we join God's club. John 16:33 says: "These things I have spoken unto you, that in me ye might have peace. In this world ye shall have tribulation; but be of good cheer; I have overcome the world."

Yes, He's overcome the world. We don't have to spend all of our time chasing after dreams or running from nightmares; all we have to do is embrace our membership in a chosen generation, a royal priesthood, a holy nation.

In declaring in 1 Peter 2:9 that saints are members of a chosen generation, a royal priesthood, a holy nation, a peculiar people, Peter uses a tiny—but powerful three-letter word: But.

Leading up to this verse, Peter says the world stumbles over Jesus and trips over the word of God, living any kind of life, a life of disobedience. Then he comes to that ninth verse and begins it with the conjunction "but."

The world might behave and believe in a manner that is contrary to God's and denies the power of the gospel, but not you, Peter tells the saints. "But you are a chosen generation, a royal priesthood, an holy nation, a peculiar people." You're different. You're in the world but not of the world.

"But," Peter says. "But" can change your direction in life. "But" can take you from a sure path to hell to the very gates of heaven. You might not know where you're headed in life right now, but when God begins speaking "buts" into your life, I dare say, when God *butts* into your life, miraculous change will come.

Daniel would surely have been the lions' dinner until God butted in. Shadrach, Meschach and Abednego were destined to be burned to a crisp until God butted in. Joseph's fate would have been that of a slave, prisoner or worse had God not butted in. In Genesis 50:20, Joseph said: "But as for you, ye thought evil against me: *but* God meant it unto good . . ."

Indeed, God kept them all safe that they might be a holy nation unto Him. And their stories are contained in the Holy Scriptures as testimonies to what God did in and through them and can still do in and through us. Dear saints, follow the example of a 6-year-old and pray. Pray that God keeps us "safe for a holy nation."

Chapter 3

'We Identify You'

"For in him we live, and move, and have our being;

as certain also of your own poets have said,

For we are also his offspring."

Acts 17:28

One of Alexander's favorite lines from the first day I heard him pray has been: "Lord, we identify you."

I've always been struck by how children are so pure and so honest and so—willing to do what many of us won't do: Be original. Be authentic. Speak to God directly and from the heart. He knows where you are and what your heart's desire is.

"We identify you."

That's like saying, "Lord we know who you are."

"We know who we are in relation to you."

That suggests that we've tried Him and know He's all right. It suggests that we have some insight into the essence of God, not just because we heard it somewhere, but on some level, we've connected and we know who He is.

It's one thing to hear and know of someone else's testimony. That encourages us and gives us hope that if God did it for them, He'll do the same for us. But when we say He's Jehovah-Jireh, we've got to know that He will provide, not because of stories momma told us or because of someone else's testimony, but because we've tried Him and know He will come through.

The fact is that Abraham wouldn't have known God was the provider He is if the Lord had not provided the ram in the bush that spared him from taking the life of Isaac, his son, as a sacrifice. When God sustains someone else, we can rejoice with them, but when He sustains us, He's our provider, our savior, our waymaker, our rock, our sword, our shield, and we react in a totally different way. When He moves for us personally, we begin to not only identify Him, but we begin to identify with Him.

When we call him Jehovah-Rapha, we've got to know He's a healer. When we declare Him Jehovah-Shalom, we've got to know that He indeed is our peace.

It's not about having a name to call God; it's about knowing unequivocally who He is in relation to us: We must be able to declare, "We identify you." It's one thing to know someone's name; it's another thing to so know their character, attributes and personality that you can readily and without hesitation identify them, their work and their presence in your life.

Our ability to identify God is indelibly linked to our faith walk. For God to be active and moving in our lives, we must trust and believe in Him. Hebrews 11:6 says: "But without faith it is impossible to please him: for he that cometh to God must believe that he is, and that he is a rewarder of them that diligently seek him."

When we identify God, we draw closer to Him; we don't separate ourselves from Him. We discern who He is in relation to our own existence because we know that we are because He is and has always been.

We forgo who we are or who we think we are and become who He wants us to be. We forget about ourselves and concentrate on Him. We allow Him to shape and mold us and have free reign in our lives.

God's biggest problem with His people, dating all the way back to the Garden and throughout His dealings with Israel, is that many forgot Him and in the process forgot who they were. And, I fear, so many today have forgotten and don't know who they are.

In Genesis, after the fall, God asks Adam: "Where art thou?"

Adam had changed. Adam had removed himself from God's presence, forgotten who he was. We are who we are because of our unique relationship with God. Without Him, we lose all sense of who we are because we lack purpose.

In Hosea 4:6, God says that Israel not only had rejected knowledge but had forgotten His law. His response was that He would not only reject them but He would forget their children. The people of Israel essentially had forgotten who they were. They had lost their identity and, as such, were not acting like God's people and were ensuring that the generation to follow them wouldn't know their identity either.

When we forget who we are, we don't act like the Father. We don't do and think and say those things that are pleasing in His sight.

We as parents often remind our children who they are and what we expect of them when they go to school, church and elsewhere. Many remind their children that they're a Jones or a Smith and that they must uphold the Jones or Smith name.

They expect them to act like they belong to the family that bore, nurtured and reared them.

I'm reminded of the prodigal son. Most of us have some of the same tendencies found in this lost young man.

His familiar story is found in Luke 15:11-32. This son goes to his father and asks for his inheritance, which he isn't supposed to get until his father dies. The boy goes off, living it up. He spends all his money on women and partying. Not only does he end up flat broke, but a famine—a recession—grips the land, and he finds himself in dire straits. He goes and gets a dead-end job feeding pigs. He falls so far until he longs to fill his stomach with the husks that the pigs ate.

He had a good father, a loving father, a giving father, a nurturing father, a father who provided for him, who took care of him, who protected him—a father he could go to in time of need or trouble. Yet, he wanted to go his own way.

God also loves us. He nurtures us. He's our provider, our waymaker, our deliverer, the bishop and keeper of our souls. But still we sometimes go our own way, putting other things before God, looking to jobs and creditors to help us live a better life. And when tough times come, when a recession hits, we get depressed. We act as the world acts. We act like people without hope. We don't know who we are.

And I'm sure many parents can see characteristics of their children in this wayward, selfish, self-centered son. But do you see yourself responding to your children even as the prodigal son's father ultimately responded to him? Or as God ultimately responds to us?

While the prodigal son had fallen to his lowest point, Luke 15:17 reveals that a great shift occurs. It says that "he came to himself." He realized that he had become something and someone very different than who his father had raised him to be. He wasn't supposed to be in this situation. He realized that even the servants at his father's house lived better than he was living. He got himself together and went home to his father and said "Father, I have sinned against heaven, and in thy sight, and am no more worthy to be called thy son." He had gone from having lost his rightful place in life to feeling he wasn't even worthy of it. But his father took him back, restored him, fell on his neck, and kissed him, put his best robe on him and put a ring on his finger and shoes on his feet.

At its core, this is about identity. The prodigal son never would have been restored if he had not come to himself and realized who he was and who his father was. Not only that, but the father was more than willing to remind the son who he was. When the son admitted his wrong and returned, the father placed upon him all those things associated with who he had raised, prepared and made possible for his son to be.

God has called each and every one of his children forth. He has given us purpose and promise. He has seated us in heavenly places with Christ Jesus. He has given us a position in his kingdom, numbered us among his children. But there are times when we, just like the prodigal son, stray from the place and position that the Father has carved out for us. And when we go our own way in that manner, we lose sight of who we are; we lose our very identity.

Many rightly note that when the prodigal son "came to himself," he snapped out of it; he recognized the error of his ways. But in addition to him getting his act together spiritually and attitude-wise, a physiological shift or move had to take place in this son's life.

He didn't simply snap out of it and realize the error of his ways, but he physically got up from out of his mess and moved away from the wrong position he had established for himself, a position in which his father had not placed him. So many people have a so-called spiritual awakening but never move out of the situation or mess that they're in.

If you've studied the miracles of Jesus, then you know that it wasn't enough for Jesus to pronounce a paralytic healed. It wasn't enough for Him to tell the paralytic to take up his bed. But, indeed, He told him to take up his bed and walk; move, do something. Get away from the place of your bondage. Move forward and become productive.

The prodigal son physically had to go back to his father and assume the position that his father had created for him. Not until he returned to the father would he realize who he really was.

We sometimes move so far away from God that we don't recognize who we are. People end up alcoholics and drug addicts and thieves, not simply because they made mistakes, but because they don't know who they are.

But if we would come to ourselves and recognize that God created us in His own image, and that He has a plan for our lives, then we will recognize who we are and assume our rightful identity as children of God. God didn't make drunks and prostitutes and adulterers and whoremongers. He didn't make gamblers and embezzlers and fornicators and gossips.

He made us—by his own power—to be like Him. We're fearfully and wonderfully made.

"We identify you," Alexander said. In order for us to consistently identify who we are and identify God as well as identify with God, we must constantly walk in who we are.

Weekly, I take the time out to remind Alexander and Christopher who they are and the promise that is on their lives. Most times, I talk to them one-on-one, but there are also times that I talk to the two of them together.

I'll tell them to look me in the eye and I'll tell them that I love them, Mom loves them, and, most of all, God loves them. "God called you from the foundation of the world, Alexander and Christopher. He put purpose and promise in your life. He has a plan for you and intends to prosper you. He knows the thoughts he thinks of you, thoughts of peace and not evil that you will have a future and a hope." (Jeremiah 29:11)

I tell them God will equip them to excel in elementary, middle and high school. They'll excel in college and will become leaders, CEOs. They will love God, love His word, and love His people. "Alexander and Christopher, you'll love your wives and love your families."

"Leaders of the city will seek you out for good godly counsel. You'll stand in the gates of the city and declare what thus saith the Lord."

Then I tell them to repeat after me: "I'm the head and not the tail, above and not beneath, well and not sick, blessed and not cursed, rich and not poor, a success and not a failure. I'm blessed in the city and blessed in the field. Blessed going out and blessed coming in. I'm a member of a chosen generation, a royal priesthood, a holy nation, a peculiar people, bought with the blood of Jesus. I'm the king's kid. Thank you, God, for blessing me."

"That, Alexander and Christopher, is who you are."

And that's who I am and who you—dear reader—and your children are. Walk in it, knowing that your identity isn't determined by your worldly position, your money or your family name. No, it's determined by the quality of your relationship with God.

Look to God and declare, as Alexander does: "Lord, we identify you."

Chapter 4

'I Want To Pray'

"Pray without ceasing."

1 Thessalonians 5:17

After the horrific earthquake in 2010 took the lives of tens of thousands of Haitians and left many orphaned, maimed, homeless, hungry and destitute, Alexander was particularly concerned about the plight of the children and their families.

He would watch the evening news to get the latest update. When they talked about it at school, he'd come home and share it with me.

Above all, he prayed. He prayed for Haiti every day—sometimes twice a day.

And it wasn't simply, "Lord, bless Haiti." He prayed for the children and for the people. He prayed graphically and specifically. "Bless the people who don't have anything to eat and have to search trash cans for food." "Bless the people whose houses were shaken down when the earthquake came." "Bless those who are hurt." "Bless those who are dying." "Lord, bless us so we can get in our car and go help the people."

Although time has passed and we don't get as much news out of Haiti these days, the people and children of that country are still in need of prayer, support and resources. They remain on Alexander's mind and in his prayers.

Likewise, he has so many others on his mind. When I listen to him pray for his mother and father and brother as well as his teachers and classmates and family and the man from the store or the lady he saw in the mall or the man who doesn't have a house, I'm always moved. I can only hope that my prayers are as pure and unselfish.

"Lord, bless those who have something to eat and those who don't have anything to eat."

"Bless those with houses and those who don't have houses."

"Help those who don't have houses to get houses."

"Bless those who have cars and those who don't have cars."

He is as genuine in his prayer for Haiti or the homeless or the sick or the person involved in an accident we might pass as he is about the prayer for his mother.

I don't recall exactly when it was that Alexander began to pray openly. It seems he's always done so.

We always pray before we leave home in the morning and after reading at night, prior to going to bed.

One morning, as we were getting ready to embark upon our day, Alexander—about 3 at the time—said, "I want to pray." From that day forward, he became our resident petite prayer warrior.

Alexander would listen to VeggieTales and other children-oriented gospel and uplifting songs in the mornings on the way to school and on the way back home. His school would reinforce what we taught at home by holding devotion, teaching them grace, etc.

When Alexander first began school at age 2, his teacher learned that he had a love for music, particularly worship songs. When Alexander got to class, they'd say, "Alexander's here. It's time for praise and worship."

In fact, many times, his mother and I wouldn't have been able to leave him at school and go to work if teachers didn't distract Alexander with praise and worship.

He continues to be attracted to praise and worship and singing; he's on the children's choir and takes drum lessons. He's also beginning to memorize Scripture. We began with five verses I was led to teach him. We not only work on memorization, but I take the time to teach him the meaning of the verses. They're Scriptures a little boy can cling to as he continues to grow with God:

- John 3:16: "For God so loved the world, that he gave his only begotten Son, that whosoever believeth in him should not perish, but have everlasting life."

- 1 Corinthians 15:10a: "But by the grace of God, I am what I am . . ."
- James 4:17: "Therefore, to him that knoweth to do good, and doeth it not, to him it is sin."
- 1 John 4:4b: "Greater is he that is in you (me), than he that is in the world."
- Philippians 4:13: "I can do all things through Christ which strengtheneth me."

The Bible tells us that a man ought always to pray. So must a child. When mom and dad are not around, when difficult decisions must be made in the face of peer pressure, when temptations are closing in, it's important for youngsters to be able to call on the Father to help them choose the right road.

As we have learned and discussed God's word, Alexander's prayers—those pure, open-book, truthful, no-pretense prayers of a child—are becoming more fervent. Without any direction to, he is beginning to include some of these Scriptures in his prayers. Just like he reminds me of promises I make to him, Alexander is learning to remind God of His promises. There is power in that: In Isaiah 55:11, God tells us He will not allow His word to return to Him void, "but it shall accomplish that which I please, and it shall prosper in the thing whereto I sent it." Indeed, God will watch over His word to perform it (Jeremiah 1:12).

Saints, teach your children to pray, to call on God, who shaped and formed them and gave them purpose and promise in this life. Prayer isn't simply quiet meditation or an exercise in positive protestations to help you through the day. Prayer is talking to and communing with an Almighty God who can keep and direct you, who can save and deliver, who can grant favor, open doors and protect. It's an opportunity to have a sincere and open discussion with a God who forgives.

Alexander believes in the power of prayer. When he had done something wrong and was about to be chastised—probably spanked at this point—by his mom, Alexander paused and said, "Let's pray."

OK, so he also has a sense of humor.

But I'll never forget one morning in particular when we were praying before leaving home for the day. The prayer that day was especially spirited. Afterward, I took Alexander out to place him in the car. When we got to the car and I had strapped him into his seat, there was Alexander, his hands still folded and his eyes still closed. His little lips were still moving.

Was he still interceding on someone's behalf or was he praying because he didn't trust my driving? I don't know. I was just glad he felt comfortable talking to the Father—and that we were delivered to our destinations safely.

When we pass by accidents on the road, Alexander prays for those involved.

When he was as young as 3, if he heard someone talking about not feeling well he'd pray for that person at night without being prompted.

As I noted in an earlier chapter, during his kindergarten year in public school, Alexander volunteered a prayer for a faculty member whose leg was bothering her. He told her that at the school he had attended in pre-school they would pray for people who needed help and healing.

One evening, we went to visit a family member who had had a leg amputated. Before we left, Alexander prayed for her, asking God to "Bless my auntie so that she can run and do the things she always could do."

Again, a prayer that many adults wouldn't pray. But the fact is that's what we want for people who have had such a difficult procedure. We do want them to run in spirit, run in faith, run in hope and, yes, run literally because they're encouraged and energized to not give up, but to press to acquire and learn to use artificial limbs that will allow them to be as mobile as possible.

When children pray, they aren't hindered by some of the negative experiences that prevent adults from being effective in prayer. Children still have imagination, still have hope, still think all things are possible. They're not ultra-educated and cerebral, trying to reason and figure things out as if they can do everything for themselves.

Children's lives aren't so filled with failures and rejections that they've decided that some things just aren't for them, that the way things are is the way they should be. Their capacity to believe is such that once they decide something is true, it takes moving heaven and earth to convince them otherwise.

Teach your child to believe in and trust in God and even if there is a time they stray, you had better believe they will return to the Father. You know, train your child up the way he or she should go and when they get older—that's right—they'll return to what they know, trust and believe in.

Alexander early on received the existence of God. While he had questions about God, he never questioned His existence.

For him to conceive of God and be earnest in prayer is natural. Whatever or whomever is on Alexander's heart to pray for, he just does it.

Prayer is meant to be uncensored, uncut, frank conversation and confession before God.

While we adults might still be hung up on what God might think of us—as if he doesn't already know everything—kids don't have such inhibitions. They pray naked prayers, even laying family concerns bare before God, whether mom and dad are listening or not. Want to clear the air of some stuff? Have family prayer and allow your children to pray.

Children aren't ashamed about admitting what they've done—or what you've done—and asking for forgiveness. That's a good thing. Confession is good for the soul and it clears the air and makes things right with God so that He will not only hear but answer your prayer.

Chapter 5

'Did You See Me On The Cross?'

"I am crucified with Christ, nevertheless I live; yet not I, but Christ liveth in me; and the life which I now live in the flesh I live by the faith of the Son of God, who loved me, and gave himself for me."

Galatians 2:20

The day before Easter 2010, Alexander, then age 4, took my understanding of Jesus' sacrifice on the cross to another level.

We had taken Alexander to church to practice for the Easter program scheduled for that Sunday as well as to participate in the church's egg hunt. Naturally, he, like all of the other children present, was excited about the egg hunt most of all.

The younger kids were allowed to begin the hunt a minute or so ahead of the older, swifter kids to give them a fighting chance to gather eggs. Alexander was among the younger kids. He dashed ahead like everyone else and quickly began dropping eggs into his basket.

Some of the eggs were in plain sight, and as we turned the corner at the front of the church, there was a tree with about four or five eggs sitting beneath it.

"You see those, Alexander?"

"Yes," he said. His eyes lit up.

Excited myself, I started walking toward the tree. But I soon realized that Alexander was headed in a different direction. I turned and asked him where he was going.

He was just a couple steps from dropping even more eggs in his basket (there was a prize for collecting the most, and some of the candy-filled plastic eggs had special prizes inside as well), but was drawn away by something else.

That something else was the cross.

Alexander walked up to the three crosses in front of our church and laid himself upon the middle cross, the one symbolic of that on which Jesus gave the ultimate sacrifice.

After a few minutes at the cross, Alexander came back and we resumed the egg hunt. Of course, the eggs that were under the tree had been snatched up.

Then Alexander made a profound impression on his father.

"Dad, did you see me on the cross?"

"Yes. What were you doing?"

He told me he wanted to be like Jesus.

Wow. Did I see him on the cross? What a question, I thought.

Before I knew it, I was asking myself, "Do I see *me* on the cross?"

That's a good question for us all to ask.

After all, we were all there 2,000 years ago. Our sins were there. Our burdens were there. Our hurt and pain were there.

Yet Jesus was on the cross. It should have been me. It should have been you. It should have been all humanity.

Alexander, fully embracing Jesus, managed to do something many who have walked with Jesus for years have failed to do: recognize that while Jesus went to the cross, He was in our place.

Needless to say, I can't imagine my son or me choosing to be on any cross. Yet, because of Alexander, I understand the need to see me on the cross. I need to see my son and family members and friends on the cross, just to understand how far God went and how powerful a sacrifice it was.

I believe that if we could see ourselves on the cross we would much better understand Jesus' work on the cross. If we could see ourselves on the cross, we would understand why it had to be Jesus and not us. If we could see ourselves on the cross, we'd get out of some of those dead-end situations we put ourselves in, we would give up that sin we so easily commit, we would better understand the sacrifice Jesus made for us and embrace the sacrifices He expects of us.

As I reflect on that Easter egg hunt, Alexander made a sacrifice of his own that day. He chose to forgo a stash of Easter eggs to go to the cross. Giving up those eggs was but a small sacrifice, for sure. But for a kid to turn away from those prized eggs at that moment spoke a truth to me.

Let's be real. For many, Easter is about the eggs, the jelly beans, fresh new clothes, ham, tradition. But that's not what Jesus, the Messiah, was about. Sacrifice and eternal glory occupied his mind. He went to the cross to save us.

"Dad, did you see me on the cross?" Alexander had asked.

Thank God that He preferred not to see us on the cross but yielded His holy son on the cross, a perfect sacrifice for imperfect people.

Next to the obvious gift of Jesus' death, burial and resurrection—the salvation of man—the lesson He taught us about sacrifice is tantamount.

Think for a moment: When was the last time you made a real sacrifice? Put someone else's interest ahead of your own? Took the wrong to quell a squabble when you knew you were right? Let others go ahead of you even if they hadn't earned it or deserved it? Shared with someone because you had been blessed with plenty? We're implored by the Bible to look on and be concerned *about the things of others* and not just our own well being.

Jesus summed it up this way in Mark 12:30-31: "And thou shalt love the Lord thy God with all thy heart, and with all thy soul, and with all thy mind, and with all thy strength: this is the first commandment. And the second is like, namely this, Thou shalt love thy neighbour as thyself. There is none other commandment greater than these."

As if the Easter 2010 experience wasn't illuminating enough, a 5-year-old Alexander taught me yet another lesson almost a year later, during the 2011 Lenten season. It was yet another truth focusing on sacrifice.

Over the years, Alexander had watched as our church fasted, prayed and sought God for guidance, purification and spiritual development. In watching church members—including his mother and I—observe Lent, he had gotten a good idea of what it was all about; he often asked questions.

One morning as I was taking him to school, Alexander delivered a shocking revelation.

"Dad, I told mom I was going to give up Goldfish for Lent," he said.

I could barely keep the car in the road for laughing so hard. You see, Alexander's grandmother loved to buy him and his little brother Goldfish, a fish-shaped cheese cracker. She would buy them every so often, but Alexander didn't eat them at all and Christopher did so only sparingly.

I took the time to talk to Alexander about the importance of giving up something that you really liked or that really mattered a lot so it would be a true sacrifice. But I really didn't need to; the sneaky grin on his face told it all.

Like I said, among other attributes, my oldest son has a great sense of humor. He knew what he was proposing wouldn't be a real sacrifice. Hey, he's a kid. What was I expecting him to give up, chocolate chip cookies?

Still, his declaration about giving up Goldfish raised a personal question for me: What's my Goldfish? Were the sacrifices I called myself making for Lent really sacrifices? Or was I giving up something that really took no real effort and really was no sacrifice? How committed are saints of God about making sacrifices—whether for Lent or in other instances?

If we give up something that we don't really like, it's obvious that's not a sacrifice.

Also, if we give up something and replace it with something else (trading one candy bar for another or swearing off Coke only to splurge on iced tea, for example), then we're missing out by not allowing God to fill that void.

That's the point: creating a real void that can only be filled by God as we seek Him through prayer, meditation and service to others.

It's a lesson we should all learn from the cross.

Chapter 6

'You Know How To Get
To Heaven, Dad?'

"That if thou shalt confess with thy mouth the Lord

Jesus, and shalt believe in thine heart that God hath

raised him from the dead, thou shalt be saved. For

with the heart man believeth unto righteousness; and

with the mouth confession is made unto salvation."

Romans 10:9-10

About a month or so before Easter 2010, Alexander—4 at the time—and I were sitting at the dinner table and he asked me about heaven.

"You know how you get to heaven, Dad?"

"Yes. Do you know?"

He then tells me that you have to believe in Jesus. "I want to go to heaven," he said.

"You do? Well you have to believe on Jesus just like you said and be saved."

"Am I saved?" he asked.

"I don't know, Alexander. Do you know what you have to do to be saved?"

"Pray."

"That's right."

And before I could say anything else, he began to pray and profess his belief in Jesus Christ.

When he finished, I explained to him what he had done and we more fully discussed what it all meant. Then we prayed again, with me leading him in the prayer of salvation in which he confessed with his mouth the Lord Jesus and verbally acknowledged his belief that God raised Jesus from the dead.

All praises be to God that my son is saved.

"Alexander, you're saved and you're going to heaven."

Now, I know many people might say that he didn't know what he was doing and that he was too young to accept Christ. But the fact is that Jesus said in Matthew 19:14, "Suffer little children, and forbid them not, to come unto me: for of such is the kingdom of heaven." In Matthew 18:3, He said: "Verily, I say unto you, Except ye be converted and become as little children, ye shall not enter into the kingdom of heaven."

Many people, parents in particular, commiserate over what is termed the age of awareness and responsibility and accountability and that sort of stuff. The truth is the Bible doesn't specifically talk about an age when children are expected or should know right from wrong and, therefore, should seek forgiveness through a relationship with Christ. As I noted above, Jesus made it clear that He wanted the children to come unto Him. Still, He didn't indicate an age.

Some people say that the age is 12 because that is the age Jesus was when He went into the temple and taught. Others embrace 13 because that's the age that a Jewish male child is said to enter manhood and a ceremony is held to denote that it's time for the young man to become responsible for his actions. (The age is 12 for Jewish girls.)

I believe that children can be born again at an early age. But different people—whether young children or mature adults—grow at different paces and will come to the knowledge of the truth at different times.

My son, willingly—of his own volition—chose to receive Christ, and he is saved. He knows right from wrong. More than that, he knows that there is only one way to be forgiven of his sin and to enter heaven: Jesus.

Does Alexander need lots of guidance and continued direction? Without a doubt. He's a kid. And, believe you me, he's an active, energetic little boy who gets into scrapes, can be hard-headed and treats the world like his own playground. Anyone with young boys knows exactly what I'm talking about.

Alexander is the healthy, rambunctious little boy God made him to be. Yes, he tries my patience and gets into trouble. I have to discipline him and rein him in. He and his little brother get into arguments and disagreements. He can be stubborn.

Yes, he prays, but he plays hard and sometimes isn't as careful as he should be. Yes, he's learning Scripture, but he sometimes says things that he shouldn't. But he will learn to do better as we teach him right from wrong and hold him accountable.

He's got a lot of natural, chronological maturing to do even as he must grow spiritually. But the fact is that, when it comes to spiritual growth, a 25-year-old or 50-year-old who had never met Jesus would have much maturing to do as well.

The first thing I told Alexander was that I would continue to talk to him and read to him and teach him Scripture and help him understand his walk and guide him as he grows into the full assurance of his salvation. "But make no mistake," I told him, "you're saved."

As we ride along in the car, whether to school or elsewhere, he and I talk about Scripture and I encourage him to learn new verses.

And Christopher? I pray continually that God will move on his heart and he will be saved. Exactly when will that happen? I don't know. But I'm confident it will.

As far as people saying Alexander, Christopher or other young children are not old enough to be saved or can't understand salvation, that's simply wrong thinking. Anyone who thinks kids are too young to embrace Christ obviously has not noticed how smart and insightful many of them are today.

Have you taken a look at what we're asking kids to grasp in kindergarten lately? As kindergarteners, Alexander and his peers were expected to master elements of reading, writing, research and oral communication as well as grasp some basic concepts involving math, numbers and operations, algebra, geometry, measurements, data analysis and probability. No, they weren't challenged with high school or college composition or algebra; it was on their level. All the same, there is an expectation—one that grows as they advance—for students to grow academically and mentally.

The kindergartners were challenged to not only retell a story but to know the characters, where the story took place and important details. They were expected to know that fantasy stories are not true and to read books to learn new information and make connections to the world. They were challenged to edit writing as well as come up with their own ideas to write about. They were expected to grasp the basic concepts of math and algebra, from addition and subtraction to charting graphs.

In other words, we believe it's quite OK to expect—even demand—that 5-year-olds be able to read, and begin to write and tell stories with a beginning, middle and end, and identify cylinders and cubes, and discern what's real from what's fantasy. We believe—rightly, I might add—that these children should be able to reason and analyze and poke and prod to come to conclusions and make declarations and determinations.

But they can't grasp who God is? Who Jesus is? That they need a savior?

They can.

Don't take my word for it. One day, 3-year-old Christopher came to me and said:

"Dad, God doesn't have a body."

"He doesn't?" I asked.

"God is a spirit."

"That's right, buddy," I said, elated. "He is a spirit. And that's why the Bible says that we must worship Him in spirit and in truth."

It's a fact he reminds me of from time to time. I'm assuming he learned that at school or in children's church because we hadn't talked about it. I'm so ecstatic about how he's grasped the concept that sometimes I'll ask him, "Christopher, does God have a body?"

"No! God is a spirit."

On another occasion, during a family outing, Christopher announced: "There is just one God, not two Gods." And, just in case there was one among us who wasn't convinced, he repeated his declaration numerous times.

Don't get me wrong. Children don't just declare a belief in Christ and know it all. Adults have much to learn themselves. Our children need someone to help them gain knowledge and understanding. That's why God blessed them with parents and other caring adults, particularly pastors and preachers and teachers in local churches and ministries. The Father expects us to come to the knowledge of the truth for ourselves and then raise up godly seed that will also come to know Jesus as savior and Lord.

Fact is that while I've been walking with Jesus for some time now and while I'm a minister of the gospel, I can't tell you exactly *how* God saved me. I'm not saying that I don't understand the doctrine of salvation and the redemptive work of Christ.

What I'm saying is that I can't explain the intricacies of God's supernatural power to free me from sin, to save me and to change me. If a carpenter restores an old cabinet, I can tell you the supplies he used and how he went about stripping and sanding it and putting new stain on it. But I can't tell you about the origins, depth and composition of God's power and what makes Him who He is.

What I know and do profess is that God Is. All I know is that I trust the Father and by grace through faith in Jesus, I'm saved. I just know that by His power, God forgave me, cleaned me up and gave me the right and privilege to be a part of His holy family.

He filled me with His spirit and gifted me to serve in the kingdom. In short, I just believed and God did the work. My job now is to walk in obedience, serve and spread the gospel.

There is no algebraic equation or scientific formula that breaks down or illustrates how one's spiritual disposition is translated from darkness into the light. It's a faith-driven process that is proven through trial. When someone is saved and walking with the Lord, you see the change; you know when it's real—at least God surely does.

Alexander believes in Christ as much as I do. His faith is as real as my faith.

It's not about being able to break down the wonders of God; it's about belief in God's greatest wonder, the redemptive work of Jesus Christ.

And to those who still don't believe—in Jesus, that is—just remember: God is grace.

His grace is sufficient for Alexander. God won't leave him of forsake him. God will be with him until the end of time.

Satan might try to trip him up, but God's grace is sufficient.

There will be some people who will try to talk down his salvation, but God's grace is sufficient.

When he makes a mistake, God will be right there, waiting to renew fellowship with him just like He's awaiting any repentant saint. When a saint sins, Satan tries to dupe him into thinking that maybe he wasn't saved after all. The devil will even have the audacity to go before God and say, "See, I told you that he would bring shame on you."

But our heavenly Father will look his child in the eye and say: "My grace is sufficient for thee: for my strength is made perfect in weakness." (2 Corinthians 12:9)

What a glorious defense by the Father.

God's grace is not only sufficient for Alexander, but it's sufficient for you and for me and everyone who is willing to come unto Jesus.

Indeed. God is grace.

Chapter 7

'This Is The Salvation
That You Gave Us'

"Beloved, when I gave all diligence to write unto

you of the common salvation, it was needful for me

to write unto you, and exhort you that ye should

earnestly contend for the faith which was once

delivered unto the saints."

Jude 1:3

Though a child, Alexander is such a pure, powerful little prayer warrior. No, he doesn't use big words and doesn't pray long.

But it's powerful just the same.

One night, I was putting Alexander to bed, and as he was praying, he was saying, "Lord, help us to be good. Help us to be good. Lord, this is the salvation that you gave us."

Lord, this is the salvation that you gave us.

That's heavy. It's as if he was saying, "Lord, this salvation you gave us is a serious and weighty matter. We can't uphold it alone. Our salvation is born out of and secured by a faith not of our own creation."

God, through the death, burial and resurrection of Jesus Christ established the faith. We, through salvation, obedience and the spreading of the gospel contend for the faith. We, through our good deeds, through our standing on and for truth, through diligent service, contend for the faith.

Alexander's words, "Lord, this is the salvation that you gave us," make it clear that God is in total control and that He chose us; we didn't choose Him. "In this was manifested the love of God toward us, because that God sent his only begotten Son into the world, that we might live through him. Herein is love, not that we loved God, but that he loved us, and sent his Son to be the propitiation for our sins." (1 John 4:9-10)

Indeed, we needed a salvation that wasn't made by or conceived of by man. If it was up to man, grace would be a fleeting, wishy washy, conditional offering rather than an abounding attribute of God.

A closer examination of what Alexander prayed could lead one to say, "See, Lord, here's the salvation, here are the doctrinal truths, here is all we deal with. Here are the struggles that we have. We need your help."

We alone can't handle the salvation we're called to walk in. We needed Jesus both to provide the means of salvation as well as to keep us strong and true to the faith.

Your personal faith in terms of your trust and belief in God and "the faith," while tied together, are two different things. While we should put our personal faith firmly and unequivocally in Jesus, you can have faith in anything—from a tree to a statue to a camel. But "the faith" is the incontrovertible, impenetrable truth anchored in Jesus Christ.

Acts 6:7 says the priests were "obedient to the faith." In Acts 14:22, Paul and Barnabas encouraged disciples in the cities of

Lystra, Iconium and Antioch to "continue in the faith." Jude exhorts us to "contend for the faith."

The faith is not one of many ways, but is the one and only way. Jesus said in John 14:6, "I am the way, the truth, and the life: no man cometh unto the Father, but by me." 1 Thessalonians 5:9 tells us, "For God hath not appointed us to wrath, but to obtain salvation by our Lord Jesus Christ."

Jesus is indeed the only way, but we must fight to not only work out our own salvation but to preserve the faith. The Christian faith is under attack in so many ways these days—from without and from within. There are so many people who believe that there is another way other than Jesus Christ. Many people in the church don't believe in absolute truths and accept—even desire—a watered-down gospel that doesn't challenge them to live a life of standard dedicated to God.

The attack on the faith is so strong that Jude 1:3 implores us to "earnestly contend," meaning to fight as a combatant, to defend the faith.

That salvation Alexander speaks of is part and parcel of our faith. We must contend for the faith earnestly every day. This isn't just about us. It's about those who can be saved through our witness and defense of the faith. Jude says have compassion on some, making a difference, and with others save them with fear, pulling them from the fire.

What kind of salvation has God given us? One worth fighting for. That's why 1 Timothy 6:12 admonishes us to fight the good fight of faith.

But as we fight, let us not forget that He who brought us to this work, He who paved the way and extended to us the right and power to be sons and daughters of God will help us. We can't do this without Him. For this is the salvation that God gave us.

Chapter 8

'This Is The Day Of Forgiveness'

"This is the day which the Lord hath made;

we will rejoice and be glad in it."

Psalm 118:24

"If we confess our sins, he is faithful and just to

forgive us our sins, and to cleanse us

from all unrighteousness."

1 John 1:9

"Lord, this is the day of forgiveness."

Upon that declaration, Alexander sometimes begins to pray and ask for forgiveness and to offer prayers in general. What a pure and direct expression from the lips of a child.

Alexander, my resident theologian, clarified the fact that *today*—not tomorrow or some other preferred, deferred or delayed time in the future that we're not promised—is the day of forgiveness. It's imperative not to put off forgiveness. Ask God for forgiveness today, ask Him to cleanse you today, ask Him to guide you today.

The Bible implores us to seek God's forgiveness. 1 John 1:9 tells us that if we're honest with God and confess our sins, He's both faithful and just to forgive us of all our sins and to cleanse us of all unrighteousness.

Alexander says don't put off for tomorrow that precious thing you can do today. There is a sense of urgency in his statement.

For saints, not a day should go by without them renewing their fellowship with the Father through sincere repentance. When we turn away from sin, we turn to God. It's an ongoing process of shedding those thoughts, words and deeds that are against the word and will of the Father and receiving His forgiveness and embrace. When embraced by the Father, we have access to the power and authority needed to live a lifestyle that pleases Him.

If you have not given your life to Christ, do not allow another day to pass without taking a serious look at your circumstance and realizing that you need a savior—Jesus Christ. What if today is the day of your departure, whether by accident or sickness or some other manner? Don't leave this life without having given your life to Christ and receiving forgiveness from the Father.

Why? Because it's the best kind of insurance you can have, far better than auto or life insurance in this life. Walk in the salvation of God and receive eternal life with Him and not in the pit of hell. And the blessing is that eternal life begins on this side, in this world, and not after you die. Walk in God's love, peace and longsuffering on this side. Walk under his umbrella of safety, under the power of His anointing, in His favor on this side.

But don't delay. "This is the day of forgiveness."

Psalm 118:24 declares "This is the day which the Lord hath made; we will rejoice and be glad in it." Some rightly note that "this is the day" refers to the day representing the work that Jesus, the stone that the builders rejected, did through his death, burial and resurrection; the day the work of God in Christ would bring salvation.

I generally agree. But the fact is that we are to rejoice always in what God has done and is doing in the life of the believer. The joy of the Lord is our strength each and every day of our lives.

Indeed, it was Jesus' work on the cross and act of sacrifice that opened the door of salvation to all who believe and allows us to declare "This is the day which the Lord hath made." What better time, better day, to be saved than today, the only day—moment, really—we're guaranteed? While Christ did the work 2,000 years ago, the fact is that today is the day that many will accept that work and receive Him as Lord and savior. In other words, today is the day Christ will rise in the life of some nonbelievers, leaving them to shout "This is the day which the Lord hath made, let us rejoice and be glad in it!"

Even now, someone has the opportunity to come to Christ, someone has the opportunity to be saved, someone has the opportunity to be delivered, someone has the opportunity to be set free, someone has the opportunity to be healed. If you're unsaved, you can stop right now and acknowledge Jesus as

Lord and savior and ask God to forgive you of your sins, to save you, to take control of your life and to fill you with His spirit.

Without delay, God will save you and you will begin to walk in the joy of the Lord. Go ahead, make your own day. The time is exactly right: "This is the day which the Lord hath made."

Until I was saved, I had no idea or understanding what it was like for those who had already received Christ. The power and reality of Jesus' resurrection had not become real in my life. But, oh, when it did, I knew what it meant to sing, "This is the day that the Lord has made, let us rejoice and be glad in it."

We should all embrace today. God made this day. And like everything else He made, "It is good."

You might not feel your best. You might be facing challenges. You might have bills that are due or past due. You might be facing troubles in your marriage. You might have had friends turn their backs on you. You might have any number of concerns.

But God made this day and it indeed is a good day. If He brought you to this day, He will escort you through this day.

Consider Genesis 1:4-5a: "And God saw the light, that it was good; and God divided the light from the darkness. And God called the light Day . . ." God had said "Let there be light" and would note that the light was "good." He would then call the light, which was good, "day," which in turn must also be "good." So, the fact that today is a day that the Lord has made makes it a good day.

Christopher testifies to that almost daily. When he wakes up in the morning, even before he gets out of the bed or looks out to see whether it's sunny or a dreary, rainy day, he pronounces, "It's a beautiful day."

It's a line from a song that describes a beautiful day as one that is, among other things, sunny. But considering that he has no information to support his statement other than the fact that he wakes up to another day God has made, I can only surmise that he's just noting that any day we rise in the land of the living is a beautiful day.

And each good and beautiful day is, as Alexander would say, a good day for forgiveness. Every new day is a day of renewal. God's mercies are renewed every morning, ready to forgive, ready to revive, ready to extend God's loving kindness toward His people. And if we confess our sins, God will forgive us and cleanse us.

But we must not allow the opportunity to pass us by.

Hebrews 3:7-8 tells us, "Wherefore as the Holy Ghost saith, Today if ye will hear his voice, harden not your hearts . . ."

This day could refer to the moment when Jesus comes into our hearts and we turn ourselves around. In Luke 19, after Jesus had met Zacchaeus, others around them questioned why Jesus was with a publican, one they deemed a sinner. That causes Zacchaeus to repent on the spot. He pledged in verse 8, "Lord, the half of my goods I give to the poor; and if I have taken any thing from any man by false accusation, I restore him four fold."

Jesus' response was, "This day is salvation come to this house . . ."

When it is your day, it's your day. And it's a day in which to rejoice and be glad. But the fact is that every day is a day to repent and make our lives right with God.

Consider 2 Corinthians 6:2: "For he saith, I have heard thee in a time accepted, and in the day of salvation have I succored thee; behold, now is the accepted time; behold, now is the day of salvation."

As Alexander would say, "This is the day of forgiveness."

I still remember that Saturday in June 2011 when Alexander, Christopher and I were riding in the car, headed to church, and I was singing along with Fred Hammond's "Jesus, Be a Fence Around Me," as it played on the radio. For some reason, that song caught Alexander's attention, and he just looked at me and smiled and clapped his hands the entire time. Suddenly, his look changed and his mood shifted. He began to sob uncontrollably. Obviously, I've seen him cry many times, but this was different. My son was weeping.

I asked what was wrong and he refused to tell me; still he kept weeping. He did so for about 10 minutes.

I was taking him to church for drum lessons. After drum practice, he was more upbeat.

"Dad, you know why I was crying?"

"Why?"

"Because I was thinking about the bad things I'd done. I don't want to sin. I didn't want God to think I was bad. I told God I was sorry for doing bad things."

I hugged him and told him it was OK. That we all do bad things sometimes, but God has said that if we confess our sins

He'll forgive us. I told him the important thing was to do good from then on.

What a beautiful day that was. Thank God for His forgiveness—today and every day.

Chapter 9

'We Have All The Praise
And You Have All The Power'

"This people have I formed for myself;
they shall show forth my praise."

Isaiah 43:21

"Thou art worthy, O Lord, to receive glory and honor
and power: for thou hast created all things,
and for thy pleasure they are and were created."

Revelation 4:11

"God has spoken once; twice have I heard this;
that power belongeth unto God."

Psalm 62:11

Just as I was about to wrap up this book, Alexander acknowledged one of the most important elements of our relationship with the Father, our very purpose: praise.

One morning as we were praying before leaving home for the day, Alexander included a line in his prayer I hadn't heard him utter before. But it was one of the most powerful:

"Lord, we have all the praise and you have all the power."

Wow! Praise the Lord!

Alexander had spoken a powerful truth, one he would continue to pray every day for weeks: God indeed has all the power, every ounce. And all we can offer Him is our praise. We were created to worship Him, to give Him all honor, all glory and, yes, all the praise.

How do we praise God? Through the fruit of our lips, the clapping of our hands, the dancing of our feet. Through song and music and instruments. Through obedience to His word. Through righteous living, through love for Him and one another.

Hebrews 13:15 says, "By him therefore let us offer the sacrifice of praise to God continually, that is, the fruit of our lips giving thanks to his name."

Why do we praise God? We praise Him for His goodness. We praise Him for salvation. For His everlasting love. For His grace and His mercy. For His holiness, His kindness. Praise Him for being a healer and redeemer and keeper and provider. Praise Him for being the creator of the ends of the earth.

But the question is this: How willing are we to praise the Lord? Will we praise Him at all times, no matter where we are or who is looking? Will we praise Him on the job as well as in the church? Will we praise Him before friend and foe? Will we praise Him in want as well as in plenty?

Many don't mind praising the Father if He heals their bodies or brings their wayward child back home or releases a financial blessing into their lives. But will they offer up praise even if he doesn't shower them with blessings? Will they praise Him just because?

Paul and Silas, in Acts 16, praised God at what some might believe was a most peculiar time. They had been locked away in prison for teaching and preaching the gospel. Instead of being in despair, they praised God through song and prayer.

Acts 16:25-26 says this: "And at midnight Paul and Silas prayed, and sang praises unto God: and the prisoners heard them. And suddenly there was a great earthquake, so that the foundations of the prison were shaken: and immediately all the doors were opened, and every one's bands were loosed."

Paul and Silas praised and guess what? The Father unleashed his power. It was earthshaking, immediate and emancipating power.

Yes, indeed, we have all the praise and God has all the power. That's why we declare that when praises go up, blessings come down. God is moved by, indeed inhabits, the praises of His people. Genuine, uninhibited praise pleases

God, who then bestows His favor, His grace and His blessings upon His people.

All that we can do for the Lord is praise Him. We can't feed Him. We can't give Him anything that He doesn't have, doesn't own—or hasn't already created.

Let us not forget Psalm 24:1: "The earth is the Lord's, and the fulness thereof; the world, and they that dwell therein."

We can't out-love our God. We can't out-live Him, out-give Him or out-think Him. As a matter of fact, we can't live without Him.

I don't know about other fathers, but it does my heart exceedingly good when my sons walk up and hug me or kiss my cheek and tell me how much they love me. It encourages me to be a better, more loving and, yes, even more giving father when they tell me how much they enjoyed a moment we shared together or a trip we took or a toy I purchased.

When I hear, "Dad, will you read to me? I like it when you read to me," I'm likely to go and read five books when only two were expected.

Think of how much more God would do for His children who praise Him.

We can't offer God anything in the way of power: Psalm 62:11 says that "God has spoken once; twice have I heard this; that power belongeth unto God." And Romans 13:1 tells us that no one gains power or authority in and of themselves, but it is given and ordained by God, "For there is no power but of God."

And as Alexander so candidly and correctly puts it: "God's power never runs out."

No, never.

That said, there is something that we, as His children, can certainly offer the Father: our praise.

When we enter into worship, praise is what we bring to the party; God does all the rest. As a matter of fact, Psalm 33:1 says "Rejoice in the Lord, O ye righteous; for praise is comely for the upright." In other words, praise looks good on you. And when God sees you draped in praise, He releases His power in your life. When you offer genuine praise, you invite God to step into the midst of the situations, circumstances and challenges you face in life.

Paul and Silas praised; God joined their prison experience and released his power in a miraculous way. Paul and Silas displayed all the praise and God displayed all the power.

That story stands as an amazing testament to the power of sincere, God-centered praise. Uninhibited praise becomes inhabited praise because it ushers in the presence of the all-powerful God.

Psalm 50 clearly illustrates Alexander's assertion that we possess the praise and God possesses all the power.

In it, God declares that every beast of the forest belongs to Him as well as the cattle on a thousand hills. He says, "I know all the fowls of the mountains: and the wild beasts of the field are mine."

He goes on to say that "If I were hungry, I would not tell thee: for the world is mine, and the fullness thereof."

He says that those who offer thanksgiving and pay vows to the Most High can call upon Him in the time of trouble and He will deliver them and they shall glorify Him.

But those who choose wickedness will see another aspect of His never-ending power. He essentially tells them to consider their ways "lest I tear you in pieces, and there be none to deliver."

Finally, God says in the 23rd and culminating verse: "Whoso offereth me praise glorifieth me: and to him that ordereth his conversation aright will I show the salvation of God."

Ultimately, we are required to give God the praise. We were created for his good pleasure. We were created to worship. We were created to praise Him. Psalm 150 declares: "Let everything that hath breath praise the Lord."

While it's amazingly pleasing to see Alexander realize our position in praise and how it is aligned with God's position in power, it shouldn't come as a surprise. Children are more open to who God is and His sovereignty than many adults are. Likewise, they're more open and genuine about their relationship with God. They don't pretend, and if they're committed to something, they're fully committed.

When they commit to praise, they don't care who is looking or listening.

In Matthew 21, Jesus enters the temple, overturns tables and throws the moneychangers out. When the blind and lame came to Him, He healed them. When the scribes and chief priests saw His marvelous works and heard the children crying in the temple, saying, "Hosanna to the son of David," they became angry.

"And said unto him, Hearest thou what these say? And Jesus saith unto them, Yea; have ye never read, Out of the mouth of babes and sucklings thou hast perfected praise?" says Matthew 21:16.

Who else to deliver the powerful truth that "we have all the praise and you have all the power" but a child?

When Alexander was 2, there were times when he'd dash to the middle of the kitchen and begin shouting, feet pounding rapidly. Every now and then, he'd shout "Hallelujah!"

Now, he and Christopher love to hear gospel music and, when the spirit moves them, they begin to praise in their own way. It could be in the car or in the house or elsewhere.

I know. You're probably questioning whether they know what they're doing and why.

But their mother and I are believers and try to live as examples for them. They in turn believe, although they don't fully understand.

When they begin singing, "I've got a praise and I've got to get it out," as we do in our church services when the Spirit of God is moving, and begin to offer up praise, I don't question their sincerity. I join them. And when I get an opportunity, I talk with them about why we praise God.

I asked Alexander once, "What is worship?" He said worship is praising God, singing songs to God, giving to God, lifting up hands to God and loving God.

I felt that was pretty astute.

Then he prayed: "Lord, we have all the praise and you have all the power."

Pretty powerful.

All praises be to God.

Benediction

*"Yea, have ye never read, Out of the mouth of babes
and sucklings thou hast perfected praise."*

Matthew 21:16

It would have been easy for me to ignore Alexander's words and actions or dismiss them as the mumblings of a child. What could my busy, inquisitive 6-year-old teach me about God? A lot. And it's not surprising. After all, God has used young people throughout biblical history to lead kingdoms, reveal truth and spread the gospel. He used David. He used Daniel and the Hebrew boys. He used Timothy.

And, yes, he uses Alexander to help grow his father. I wait anxiously to see what God will reveal next through Alexander. And with Christopher, my 3-year-old, not far behind and beginning to express his own understanding of God more and more, who knows? God may well be speaking to me in full stereo soon.

So far, God has used Alexander to teach his earthly father a number of lessons about the Heavenly Father. As Alexander expressed himself, in his own words and in his own way, he has been helping me see the Father through his eyes. I also have been challenged to search the Scriptures for understanding and meaning in what Alexander has revealed.

Finally, God has given me a charge to not simply understand but to live out what has been revealed to me. I must be a good example for my boys and, above all, teach them about God's love and the saving grace of Jesus Christ.

In short, God has been growing me up so that I can not only be a better saint and servant, but also so I can be a better husband and father. He is using Alexander and Christopher to prepare me to teach and nurture these two boys he has assigned me to father.

How about you? What's God saying to you through your children and others around you? I pray that your ears are open and your spirit is receptive.

Listen to the voices around you that are revealing the Father in a fresh, compelling way. Search the Scriptures to gain a deeper meaning and apply it in your life. Ask God, through prayer, to reveal to you what it is He would have you to learn and embrace. And then live out, share and declare what thus saith the Lord.

Let us pray:

Father God in Heaven, we thank you, we praise you, we bless you, we magnify your holy and righteous name. Lord, we come desiring a closer relationship with you. We come desiring to know Jesus in the fellowship of His suffering and the power of His resurrection. We come, Lord, seeking your face and not your hand. Teach us, Father, to be attentive as you speak to us through your chosen vessels, be they our children, our family, our friends, our pastors or others. Father, we know that we serve a supernatural God who uses whom he chooses, a God who can do exceeding, abundantly above all we could ask or think. A God who sent a supernatural Savior to save a sinful world.

Teach us, Lord, to love not the world, neither the things that are in the world. Teach us to set our minds on things above and not on things on this earth. Teach us to repent of our sins, walk in forgiveness and walk humbly before you, Lord. Teach us to pray and to praise and to worship you in spirit and in truth.

Teach us to walk in obedience, to walk in sacrifice, to walk in love. Teach us to seek the things of God as precious jewels. Teach us to read and meditate on your word. Teach us to seek you in honest, sincere, transparent prayer. Teach us to turn away from those things that weigh us down spiritually and rob us of the joy of Your grace. Teach us to turn away from sin—great and small. Turn away from evil and idle thoughts. Turn away from hollow deeds and thoughtless, damaging words. Then, Lord, teach us to turn to you, the True and Living God, in forgiveness that we might be cleansed, filled with your Holy Spirit and prepared for the Master's use. Teach us to reach deep within the depths of our being, that we might lay hold to your purpose and your promise for our lives.

We pray that we develop a burning desire to know more intimately that Jesus who suffered, bled and died that we might live. We thank you for the passion and the compassion. Despite the lashes and the thorns and the blood and the pain and the abuse, it was the passion and His compassion for a dying and sinful world that drove our Lord up Golgotha's Hill. It was the passion and His compassion that compelled Him to endure the cross and the shame. It was the passion and His compassion that drove Him to give up the Ghost. It was the passion and His compassion that escorted Him to victory over death, hell and the grave. Today, it is the passion and His compassion that drive Him even now, though seated firmly on the right hand of the Father, to intercede on our behalf.

Father, we thank you for your unmerited favor. We thank you for your grace and your mercy. We thank you for not holding our sins and shortcomings against us but making a way for us to continually walk in fellowship with you. Father, we thank you that we can indeed declare that we identify you, for you are our deliverer, our waymaker, our keeper, our redeemer, our savior, our healer. You are the ancient of days, maker of the ends of the earth, the Alpha and the Omega. There's no searching of your understanding. You, indeed are our God, the God who blesses us. The God who is love. The God who is infinite. The God who is grace and whose grace is sufficient for us.

Now may the grace of our Lord Jesus Christ, the sweet communion of the Holy Spirit and the love of God rest, rule and abide with us forever and ever. It's in the name of the matchless and mighty name of Jesus, who is the Christ, we pray. Amen.